#180DaysOfPraise

📷 @NewHopeRBC + @NotYoGrandMaMasBibleStudy
📘 @NewHopeRBC + @NotYoGrandMaMasBibleStudy
🖱 www.NewHopeRBC.com

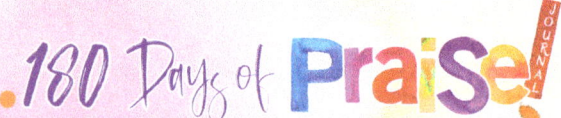

Copyright © 2025 by D Nicole Williams

All rights reserved.

No portion of this publication may be reproduced, distributed, or transmitted in any form or by any means, including photocopying, recording, or other electronic or mechanical methods, without the prior written permission of the publisher, except in the case of brief quotations embodied in critical reviews and certain other noncommercial uses permitted by copyright law.

For permission requests, email the publisher, addressed "ATTN: Permissions" at the following: NewHope@NewHopeRBC.com

Bulk discounts are available on quantity purchases by associations, corporations, and others for business, educational and ministry use. For details, contact the publisher at the address above.

ISBN: 978-1-942650-39-3

> *I will bless the Lord at all times.*
> *His praise shall continually be in my mouth.*
> — Psalm 34

Welcome to your *journey of praise*—a journey that is equal parts sacrifice, celebration, testimony, and transformation.

This journal exists so you can lift up your hands and worship God no matter what you're going through. This praise journey is for the days when praise comes easily, and especially for the days when it feels hard. As you journal through these pages, remember that, sometimes, the only thing we have is our worship. Sometimes, the only thing we have to give is our presence.

For the next 180 days, I invite you not just to record your praises to God, but to offer your praise as your testimony, your cry, and your declaration. Whether your praise contradicts the senses or offends the situation, let it be a light that draws you closer to God and inspires others. Faith and praise are muscles—you've got to work for them! And with each daily entry, you will build spiritual strength and resilience.

As you begin, remember the encouragement to praise the Lord at all times. Praise God when it's good. Praise God when it's bad. This type of praise is not for show. It is not for comfort. It is a bold witness expressing what God has done while paving the way for what God is going to do.

Let these next 180 days be your altar, where you meet God with open hands and a trusting heart.

> *"Even when you don't see it, see it.*
> *Even when you don't feel it, know it by faith."*
> — Pastor D Nicole Williams

Why a praise journal for 180 days?
- Because many are the afflictions of the righteous, but the Lord delivers them from them all.
- Because sometimes, the only way through affliction is with gratitude and rejoicing, even before the breakthrough arrives.
- Because God is worthy to be praised at all times—when it's good and when it's bad, when it's up and when it's down, when you smile and when you frown.

This journal is your invitation to offer up your praise, both sacrificially and joyfully, each day for 180 days. Let praise lead you into increased faith and gratitude.

Ultimately, faith should move you to praise. Despite what it feels like, praise God, realizing that praise is a sacrifice. As you move through moments of doubt, loss, hope, and victory, journal... in faith. Pray... in faith. Praise... in faith.

> "Praise offends doubt, praise offends fear, praise offends hopelessness, helplessness, defeat."
> - Pastor D Nicole Williams

Begin each day knowing that praise will strengthen you! Praise God for what you cannot yet see. Praise Him in advance! Don't worry about what anyone else is doing, who's watching you, who's judging you, or who is unsure. Your praise has nothing to do with how you or anyone else feels... Your praise has everything to do with who our God is!

May each entry be a celebration of what God has done and a prophecy of what He will do next. As you reach for 180 days of praise, expect joy, healing, and a 180° transformation! Because when you're giving thanks at all times, this is God's will for you in Christ Jesus.

Welcome to your praise journey!

My Prayer to Guide this 180 Day Journey

Before you begin, consider your hopes, dreams, and desperate desires for this process. Let this prayer address your urgent need for change and spiritual growth.

Pains and Problems and Problem People

We begin with a simple process of lament to lay our burdens down. Because this journal has no additional space to grumble or murmur, let's lay it all out on the table here and watch God transform our views over the next 180 days.

- ☐
- ☐
- ☐
- ☐
- ☐
- ☐
- ☐
- ☐
- ☐
- ☐
- ☐

i PRAISE God for...

Month:

SUN	MON	TUE	WED	THU	FRI	SAT

And...

Month:

SUN	MON	TUE	WED	THU	FRI	SAT

Month:

SUN	MON	TUE	WED	THU	FRI	SAT

Month:

SUN	MON	TUE	WED	THU	FRI	SAT

Points of Praise

Brainstorm areas of praise that you need to visit throughout this journey. Then, on those days when praise is hard, come back to this list for inspiration on what you can praise God for.

☐
☐
☐
☐
☐
☐
☐
☐
☐
☐
☐

My Prayer for Transformation as I Journey

Compose a prayer focused on your transformation needs as you shift to more praise.

Praise #   Date

- [ ] The BLESSINGS,
- [ ] The FAVOR,
- [ ] The GOODNESS,
     of God

- The BLESSINGS.
- The FAVOR.
- The GOODNESS.
  of God

 Praise #  Date

☐ The BLESSINGS,
☐ The FAVOR,
☐ The GOODNESS,
   of God

Praise #   Date

☐ The BLESSINGS.
☐ The FAVOR.
☐ The GOODNESS.
       of God

- [ ] The BLESSINGS.
- [ ] The FAVOR.
- [ ] The GOODNESS.
of God

- The BLESSINGS.
- The FAVOR.
- The GOODNESS.
     ...of God

 # Praise

Date

- [ ] The BLESSINGS.
- [ ] The FAVOR.
- [ ] The GOODNESS.

of God

- The BLESSINGS.
- The FAVOR.
- The GOODNESS.
  of God

Praise # _____   Date _____

- [ ] The BLESSINGS.
- [ ] The FAVOR.
- [ ] The GOODNESS.
  of God

- [ ] The BLESSINGS.
- [ ] The FAVOR.
- [ ] The GOODNESS.

of God

Praise #

Date

☐ The BLESSINGS.
☐ The FAVOR.
☐ The GOODNESS.
  of God

 #

Date

- [ ] The BLESSINGS.
- [ ] The FAVOR.
- [ ] The GOODNESS.
  ### of God

Praise #   Date

☐ The BLESSINGS,
☐ The FAVOR,
☐ The GOODNESS,
   of God

 Praise #

 Date

- [ ] The BLESSINGS.
- [ ] The FAVOR.
- [ ] The GOODNESS.
  ### of God

- The BLESSINGS,
- The FAVOR,
- The GOODNESS

of God

- The BLESSINGS.
- The FAVOR.
- The GOODNESS.

of God

- [ ] The BLESSINGS.
- [ ] The FAVOR.
- [ ] The GOODNESS.
  of God

- [ ] The BLESSINGS.
- [ ] The FAVOR.
- [ ] The GOODNESS.
    of God

- [ ] The BLESSINGS.
- [ ] The FAVOR.
- [ ] The GOODNESS.
   ### of God

☐ The BLESSINGS.
☐ The FAVOR.
☐ The GOODNESS.
of God

 Praise #   Date

☐ The BLESSINGS.
☐ The FAVOR.
☐ The GOODNESS.
     of God

Praise # _____ Date _____

- [ ] The BLESSINGS.
- [ ] The FAVOR.
- [ ] The GOODNESS.
   of God

- The BLESSINGS.
- The FAVOR.
- The GOODNESS.
  of God

 #  Date

- [ ] The BLESSINGS.
- [ ] The FAVOR.
- [ ] The GOODNESS.
    of God

How has my understanding of praise shifted since I began this journey?

 # Praise

 Date

- [ ] The BLESSINGS.
- [ ] The FAVOR.
- [ ] The GOODNESS.
   of God

- [ ] The BLESSINGS.
- [ ] The FAVOR.
- [ ] The GOODNESS.
  of God

Praise # .... Date ....

☐ The BLESSINGS.
☐ The FAVOR.
☐ The GOODNESS.
       of God

Praise #　　　　　　　　　　　　　　　　　　　**Date**

☐ The BLESSINGS
☐ The FAVOR
☐ The GOODNESS
　　　of God

Praise#  Date

- [ ] The BLESSINGS.
- [ ] The FAVOR.
- [ ] The GOODNESS.
of God

- [ ] The BLESSINGS.
- [ ] The FAVOR.
- [ ] The GOODNESS.

of God

Praise #   Date

- [ ] The BLESSINGS.
- [ ] The FAVOR.
- [ ] The GOODNESS.
  ### of God

Praise #   Date

- [ ] The BLESSINGS.
- [ ] The FAVOR.
- [ ] The GOODNESS.
       of God

 # Praise

 Date

- [ ] The BLESSINGS.
- [ ] The FAVOR.
- [ ] The GOODNESS.
  of God

☐ The BLESSINGS.
☐ The FAVOR.
☐ The GOODNESS.
　　　　　of God

Praise#   Date

- [ ] The BLESSINGS.
- [ ] The FAVOR.
- [ ] The GOODNESS.
  ### of God

☐ The BLESSINGS.
☐ The FAVOR.
☐ The GOODNESS.
　　　　.of God

- The BLESSINGS.
- The FAVOR.
- The GOODNESS.
  of God

PraiSe

Date

☐ The BLESSINGS.
☐ The FAVOR.
☐ The GOODNESS.
   of God

Praise # _____ Date _____

☐ The BLESSINGS,
☐ The FAVOR,
☐ The GOODNESS,
of God

Praise # _____ Date _____

- [ ] The BLESSINGS.
- [ ] The FAVOR.
- [ ] The GOODNESS.
  of God

Praise #  Date

- [ ] The BLESSINGS.
- [ ] The FAVOR.
- [ ] The GOODNESS.
  ### of God

Praise

Date

- [ ] The BLESSINGS.
- [ ] The FAVOR.
- [ ] The GOODNESS.

of God

Date

☐ The BLESSINGS.
☐ The FAVOR.
☐ The GOODNESS.
  of God

Praise #   **Date**

☐ The BLESSINGS.
☐ The FAVOR.
☐ The GOODNESS.
　　　　of God

- The BLESSINGS.
- The FAVOR.
- The GOODNESS.

of God

How has my faith grown since starting this journey of reflection and praise?

- The BLESSINGS.
- The FAVOR.
- The GOODNESS.
  ### of God

- The BLESSINGS.
- The FAVOR.
- The GOODNESS.
  of God

- The BLESSINGS.
- The FAVOR.
- The GOODNESS.
  of God

Praise #   Date

- [ ] The BLESSINGS.
- [ ] The FAVOR.
- [ ] The GOODNESS.
  ### of God

- The BLESSINGS,
- The FAVOR,
- The GOODNESS,

of God

Praise # _____ Date _____

☐ The BLESSINGS.
☐ The FAVOR.
☐ The GOODNESS.
   of God

 # Praise

 Date

- The BLESSINGS.
- The FAVOR.
- The GOODNESS.
  of God

☐ The BLESSINGS.
☐ The FAVOR.
☐ The GOODNESS.
      of God

Praise # _____ Date _____

- The BLESSINGS,
- The FAVOR,
- The GOODNESS,

of God

Praise

Date

- [ ] The BLESSINGS.
- [ ] The FAVOR.
- [ ] The GOODNESS.

of God

 Praise #

 Date

- [ ] The BLESSINGS.
- [ ] The FAVOR.
- [ ] The GOODNESS.
of God

Praise #   Date

- The BLESSINGS.
- The FAVOR.
- The GOODNESS.
  of God

 Praise #  Date

- [ ] The BLESSINGS.
- [ ] The FAVOR.
- [ ] The GOODNESS.
    of God

 Praise #

Date

☐ The BLESSINGS.
☐ The FAVOR.
☐ The GOODNESS.
   of God

Praise #   **Date**

☐ The BLESSINGS.
☐ The FAVOR.
☐ The GOODNESS.
        of God

- [ ] The BLESSINGS.
- [ ] The FAVOR.
- [ ] The GOODNESS.
  of God

How have I experienced God's presence or intervention in unexpected ways while reflecting on praise?

Praise # _____ Date _____

- [ ] The BLESSINGS.
- [ ] The FAVOR.
- [ ] The GOODNESS.
    of God

Praise #   Date

☐ The BLESSINGS.
☐ The FAVOR.
☐ The GOODNESS.
           of God

 Praise #  Date

☐ The BLESSINGS.
☐ The FAVOR.
☐ The GOODNESS.
　　　of God

Praise: Date:

- [ ] The BLESSINGS.
- [ ] The FAVOR.
- [ ] The GOODNESS.
  ### of God

Praise #   Date

☐ The BLESSINGS.
☐ The FAVOR.
☐ The GOODNESS.
    of God

- The BLESSINGS.
- The FAVOR.
- The GOODNESS.

of God

 # Praise#

Date

- The BLESSINGS.
- The FAVOR.
- The GOODNESS.
  ## of God

Praise

Date

- [ ] The BLESSINGS.
- [ ] The FAVOR.
- [ ] The GOODNESS.
  ### of God

Praise # _____   Date _____

☐ The BLESSINGS.
☐ The FAVOR.
☐ The GOODNESS.
　　　　of God

Praise

Date

- ☐ The BLESSINGS.
- ☐ The FAVOR.
- ☐ The GOODNESS.
  ### of God

- [ ] The BLESSINGS.
- [ ] The FAVOR.
- [ ] The GOODNESS.
    ### of God

 #

- [ ] The BLESSINGS.
- [ ] The FAVOR.
- [ ] The GOODNESS.
  of God

 Praise#

 Date

- [ ] The BLESSINGS.
- [ ] The FAVOR.
- [ ] The GOODNESS..
  of God

Praise #   Date

- [ ] The BLESSINGS,
- [ ] The FAVOR,
- [ ] The GOODNESS,
  of God

Praise #

Date

- [ ] The BLESSINGS.
- [ ] The FAVOR.
- [ ] The GOODNESS.
   of God

☐ The BLESSINGS.
☐ The FAVOR.
☐ The GOODNESS.
of God

 **Praise #**   **Date**

- The BLESSINGS.
- The FAVOR.
- The GOODNESS.
       of God

Praise # Date

- [ ] The BLESSINGS.
- [ ] The FAVOR.
- [ ] The GOODNESS.

of God

Praise#

Date

- [ ] The BLESSINGS.
- [ ] The FAVOR.
- [ ] The GOODNESS.
   ### of God

 Praise #  Date

- [ ] The BLESSINGS.
- [ ] The FAVOR.
- [ ] The GOODNESS.
  ### of God

 Praise #  Date

- [ ] The BLESSINGS.
- [ ] The FAVOR.
- [ ] The GOODNESS.
of God

☐ The BLESSINGS.
☐ The FAVOR.
☐ The GOODNESS.
      of God

 #  Date

- [ ] The BLESSINGS.
- [ ] The FAVOR.
- [ ] The GOODNESS.
  ### of God

In what ways has my view of challenges changed as a result of regular worship and praise?

Praise #   **Date**

- The BLESSINGS.
- The FAVOR.
- The GOODNESS.
  - **of God**

 #

- [ ] The BLESSINGS.
- [ ] The FAVOR.
- [ ] The GOODNESS.
  ### of God

What have I discovered about myself through the process of journaling and engaging with praise?

How has my prayer life evolved throughout this journey?

180 Days of Praise helped me

#180DaysOfPraise
Thanks for allowing us to partake in your praise journey!
@NewHopeRBC   @NotYoGrandMaMasBibleStudy   NewHopeRBC.com

www.ingramcontent.com/pod-product-compliance
Lightning Source LLC
Chambersburg PA
CBHW040000290426
43673CB00077B/288